Ark of Salvation

Ark of Salvation
Essential Islamic Beliefs & Obligations

Safīnat al-najā fī mā yajib ʿalā al-ʿabdi li-mawlāhu

Shaykh Sālim bin ʿAbd Allāh bin Sumayr al-Ḥaḍramī al-Shāfiʿī

Translation & notes by
MUSA FURBER

Ark of Salvation: Essential Islamic Beliefs & Obligations

Copyright © 2020 by Steven (Musa) Woodward Furber

Last updated: 18 January 2024

All rights reserved. Except for brief quotations in a review, this book, or any part thereof, may not be reproduced, stored in or introduced into a retrieval system, or transmitted, in any form or by any means, electronic, mechanical, photocopying, recording or otherwise, without the prior written permission of the copyright owner.

ISBN   978-1-944904-18-0 (paper)

Published by:
Islamosaic
islamosaic.com

Cover image licensed by Ingram Image

All praise is to Allah alone, the Lord of the Worlds
And may He send His benedictions upon
our master Muhammad, his Kin
and his Companions
and grant them
peace

Transliteration Key

ء	ʾ (A distinctive glottal stop made at the bottom of the throat.)	ظ	ẓ (An emphatic *th* sound, like the *th* in *this*, made behind the front teeth.)
ا	ā, a	ع	ʿ (A distinctive Semitic sound made in the middle of the throat and sounding to a Western ear more like a vowel than a consonant.)
ب	b		
ت	t		
ث	th (Pronounced like the *th* in *think*.)		
ج	j	غ	gh (A guttural sound made at the top of the throat resembling the untrilled German and French *r*.)
ح	ḥ (Hard *h* sound made at the Adam's apple in the middle of the throat.)		
خ	kh (Pronounced like *ch* in Scottish *loch*.)	ف	f
		ق	q (A hard *k* sound produced at the back of the palate.)
د	d		
ذ	dh (Pronounced like *th* in *this*.)	ك	k
		ل	l
ر	r (A slightly trilled *r* made behind the upper front teeth.)	م	m
		ن	n
		ه	h (This sound is like the English *h* but has more body. It is made at the very bottom of the throat and pronounced at the beginning, middle, and ends of words.)
ز	z		
س	s		
ش	sh		
ص	ṣ (An emphatic *s* pronounced behind the upper front teeth.)		
		و	ū, u
ض	ḍ (An emphatic *d*-like sound made by pressing the entire tongue against the upper palate.)	ي	ī, i, y
		ﷺ	A supplication made after mention of the Prophet Muḥammad, translated as "May Allah bless him and give him peace."
ط	ṭ (An emphatic *t* sound produced behind the front teeth.)		

Contents

PREFACE	VIII
Author's Introduction	1
Beliefs	3
Purification	5
Prayer	21
Funerals	51
Zakat	56
Fasting	57
Concluding Remarks	65
DETAILED TABLE OF CONTENTS	66

Preface

In the Name of Allah, Most Merciful and Compassionate

This short booklet contains a translation of Shaykh Sālim bin 'Abd Allāh bin Sumayr al-Ḥaḍramī al-Shāfi'ī (–1270 AH/1855 CE)'s *Safīnat al-najā fī mā yajib 'alā al-'abdi li-mawlāhu* (*"The Ark of Salvation: The Servant's Duties Towards His Lord,"* re-subtitled here with *"Essential Islamic Beliefs and Obligations"*). I have been asked many times whether I have translated it. I do not like turning them away empty-handed, so I decided to provide them with a quick, plain, unannotated rendering of the *Safīnah* that they could read from while following along in a lesson.

I have five editions that include the basic text, including Dār al-Minhāj's edition of Shaykh Aḥmad bin 'Umar al-Shāṭirī (1312–1360)'s commentary *Nayl al-rajā' bi-sharḥ Safīnat al-najā'* (published in 1424/2003); their edition of *Safīnat al-najāh* includes just the basic text (1430/2009); Dār Ibn Ḥazm's edition of Muḥammad Nawawī al-Jāwī al-Bantanī (1230/1815–1316/1898)'s commentary *Kāshifat al-sajā sharḥ Safīnat al-najā* (1432/2011); Dār al-Nūr's edition of Shaykh Muḥammad

Preface

ʿĀmawah's commentary *Manār al-hudā sharḥ Safīnat al-najā* (2016); and Dār al-Ḍiyā"s edition of Shaykh Aḥmad bin ʿUmar al-Shāṭirī's *Nayl al-rajā' bi-sharḥ Safīnat al-najā'* (1439/2018). Each edition gives a slightly different name for the basic text.

Since requests for the book almost always come from students reading it with an instructor, I left the book without annotations—except for a few spots where I felt a few extra words were needed. Most of the issues mentioned in this book are covered in my other books, so you can also turn to them for explanations, examples, and evidence. The author enumerated some lists using ordinal numbers. I took the liberty of enumerating most other lists, using cardinal numbers and digits.

Many thanks are owed to Asif for his generous help with cover designs and proofreading. Please say a prayer for him, his family, and his father.

Where I have succeeded, it is only through the grace of Allah. Where I have faltered, it is from my own shortcomings. May Allah forgive the author, everyone mentioned in the book, its owners, readers, listeners, and all Muslims—living and dead.

MUSA FURBER
PUTRAJAYA
APRIL 19, 2020

This page left blank

Author's Introduction

بِسمِ اللهِ الرَّحمنِ الرَّحيمِ

الحَمدُ لِلّهِ رَبِّ العالَمينَ، وبِهِ نَستَعينُ على أُمورِ الدُّنيا والدِّينِ.

اللَّهُمَّ يا هاديَ المُضِلّينَ، لا هاديَ لَهُم غَيرُك .. ﴿اِهدِنَا الصِرَاطَ المُستَقِيمَ ۝ صِرَاطَ الَّذينَ أَنعَمتَ عَلَيهِم﴾ [الفاتحة: ٦ – ٧] ﴿مِنَ النَّبِيِّينَ وَالصِّدِّيقِينَ وَالشُّهَدَاءِ وَالصَّالِحِينَ﴾ [النساء: ٦٩] ﴿غَيرِ المَغضُوبِ عَلَيهِم وَلَا الضَّالِّينَ﴾ [الفاتحة: ٧].

وصَلَّىٰ اللهُ وسَلَّمَ علىٰ سَيِّدِنا مُحَمَّدٍ خاتِمِ النَّبِيِّينَ، وعلىٰ آلِهِ وصَحبِهِ أَجمَعينَ.

ولا حَولَ ولا قُوَّةَ إِلَّا بِاللَّهِ العَلِيِّ العَظِيمِ.

In the name of Allah,
the Merciful and Compassionate

All praise is for Allah, Lord of the Worlds. We seek assistance through Him in our affairs related to this world and the afterlife.

Ark of Salvation

O Allah! O Guider of those who are misguided who have no guider other than You! Guide us to the straight path, the path of those upon whom You have favored – [the path] of the prophets, the truthful, the martyrs and the righteous – not [the path] of those who have earned Your anger or of those who go astray.

May He send His benedictions upon our master Muhammad the last of the Messengers, his kin, and his Companions one and all. And there is no motion or power except through Allah Mighty and Majestic.

Beliefs

The Pillars of Islam

(فَصلٌ) أركانُ الإسلامِ خَمسةٌ:
[١] شَهادَةُ أن لا إلَهَ إلّا اللَّهُ وأَنَّ مُحَمَّدًا رَسولُ اللَّهِ.
[٢] وإقامُ الصلاةِ.
[٣] وإيتاءُ الزكاةِ.
[٤] وصَومُ رَمَضانَ.
[٥] وحَجُّ البَيتِ مَنِ استَطاعَ إليهِ سَبيلًا.

The pillars of Islam are five:
1. testifying that there is no deity other than Allah and that Muhammad is the Messenger of Allah,
2. establishing prayer,
3. paying zakat,
4. fasting Ramadan, and
5. making the Hajj pilgrimage to the House [in Mecca] if able to do so.

The Pillars of Faith

(فَصلٌ) أَركانُ الإيمانِ سِتَّةٌ:

[١] أَن تُؤمِنَ بِاللَّهِ.

[٢] وَمَلائِكَتِهِ.

[٣] وكُتُبِهِ.

[٤] ورُسُلِهِ.

[٥] وبِاليَومِ الآخِرِ.

[٦] وبِالقَدَرِ؛ خَيرِهِ وشَرِّهِ مِنَ اللَّهِ تَعالىٰ.

The pillars of faith are six:
1. belief in Allah,
2. His Angels,
3. His revealed books,
4. His messenger,
5. the final day, and
6. that destiny (good and evil) is from Allah Most High.

The Meaning of "There Is No Deity Other Than Allah"

(فَصلٌ) ومَعنىٰ «لا إلَهَ إلّا اللَّهُ»: لا مَعبودَ بِحَقٍّ في الوُجودِ إلّا اللَّهُ.

The meaning of "Lā ilāha illa Allāh" ("there is no deity except Allah") is that nothing that exists is rightfully worshiped other than Allah.

Purification

Physical Maturity

(فَصلٌ) عَلاماتُ البُلوغِ ثَلاثٌ:
[١] تَمامُ خَمسَ عَشرَةَ سَنَةً في الذَّكَرِ والأُنثىٰ.
[٢] والاحتِلامُ في الذَّكَرِ والأُنثىٰ لِتِسعِ سِنينَ.
[٣] والحَيضُ في الأُنثىٰ لِتِسعِ سِنينَ.

The indicators of physical maturity are three:
1. a male or female completing fifteen lunar years of age,
2. a male or female experiencing a nocturnal emission [i.e., ejaculation] after nine lunar years of age, and
3. a female menstruating after nine lunar years of age.

Cleaning with Dry Objects

(فَصلٌ) شُروطُ الحَجَرِ ثَمانِيَةٌ:
[١] أَن يَكونَ بِثَلاثَةِ أَحجارٍ.
[٢] وأَن يُنَقِّيَ المَحَلَّ.
[٣] وأَن لا يَجِفَّ النَّجَسُ.

[٤] وأن لا يَنتَقِلَ.
[٥] ولا يَطرَأ عَلَيهِ آخَرُ.
[٦] ولا يُجاوِزَ صَفحَتَهُ وحَشَفَتَهُ.
[٧] وأن لا يُصيبَهُ ماءٌ.
[٨] وأن تَكونَ الأحجارُ طاهِرَةً.

The conditions for cleaning with stones [being acceptable] are eight:
1. that it be with three stones,
2. that it clean the affected area,
3–4. that the filth does not dry or transfer to another location,
5. that one not be affected by any other filth,
6. that the filth not be located beyond the buttocks or foreskin,
7. that water does not reach the filth, and
8. the stones are pure.

Obligatory Actions of Ablution

(فَصلٌ) فُروضُ الوُضوءِ سِتَّةٌ:
الأوَّلُ: النِّيَّةُ.
الثَّاني: غَسلُ الوَجهِ.
الثَّالِثُ: غَسلُ اليَدَينِ مَعَ المِرفَقَينِ.
الرَّابعُ: مَسحُ شَيءٍ مِنَ الرَّأسِ.

الخامِسُ: غَسلُ الرِّجلَينِ مَعَ الكَعبَينِ.
السَّادِسُ: التَّرتيبُ.

The obligatory actions of ablution [*wuḍū'*] are six.
The first is the intention.
The second is washing the face.
The third is washing the arms [up to and] including the elbows.
The fourth is wiping part of the head.
The fifth is washing the feet with the ankles.
The sixth is their order.

The Intention

(فَصلٌ) النِّيَّةُ: قَصدُ الشيءِ مُقتَرِنًا بِفِعلِهِ، ومَحَلُّها القَلبُ، والتَّلفُّظُ بها سُنَّةٌ، ووَقتُها عِندَ غَسلِ أَوَّلِ جُزءٍ مِنَ الوَجهِ.
والتَّرتيبُ: أَن لا يُقَدَّمَ عُضوٌ علىٰ عُضوٍ.

Intention is directing [oneself] to perform something concurrent to its performance.

Its place is the heart.

Uttering it is a Sunnah.

Its time [when making ablution] is when washing the first part of the face.

The order [during ablution] is not putting one limb before another.

Large And Small Volumes of Water

(فَصلٌ) الماءُ قَليلٌ وكَثيرٌ. القَليلُ: ما دونَ القُلَّتَينِ، والكَثيرُ:

قُلَّتَانِ فَأَكْثَرُ.

والقَلِيلُ يَتَنَجَّسُ بِوُقوعِ النَّجاسَةِ فيهِ؛ وإن لَم يَتَغَيَّر.

والكَثِيرُ لا يَتَنَجَّسُ إلّا إذا تَغَيَّرَ طَعمُهُ أو لَونُهُ أو ريحُهُ.

Water can be small and large volumes. A small volume is what is less than two *qullah*s. A large volume is two or more *qullah*s [approximately 216 liters or 57.1 US gallons].

A small volume becomes filthy by the presence of filth in it – even if it does not change.

A large volume does not become filthy unless its taste, color, or smell changes.

The Purification Bath
Occasions That Require It

(فَصْلٌ) مُوجِباتُ الغُسلِ سِتَّةٌ:

[١] إيلاجُ الحَشَفَةِ في الفَرجِ.

[٢] وخُرُوجُ المَنِيِّ.

[٣] والحَيضُ.

[٤] والنِّفاسُ.

[٥] والوِلادَةُ.

[٦] والمَوتُ.

The occasions that obligate a purificatory bath are six:

1. insertion of the glans into the vagina,
2. discharge of ejaculate,

Purification

3. menstruation,
4. postnatal bleeding,
5. birth, and
6. death.

Obligatory Actions of The Purificatory Bath

(فَصلٌ) فُروضُ الغُسلِ اثنانِ:

[١] النِّيَّةُ.

[٢] وتَعميمُ البَدَنِ بالماءِ.

The obligatory acts of the purificatory bath are two:
1. the intention, and
2. covering the entire body with water.

Ablution
Prerequisites for Ablution

(فَصلٌ)
شُروطُ الوُضوءِ عَشَرَةٌ:

[١] الإسلامُ.

[٢] والتَّمييزُ.

[٣] والنَّقاءُ عَنِ الحَيضِ والنِّفاسِ.

[٤] وعَمَّا يَمنَعُ وُصولَ الماءِ إلى البَشَرَةِ.

[٥] وأن لا يَكونَ علىٰ العُضوِ ما يُغَيِّرُ الماءَ.

[٦] والعِلَمُ بِفَرْضِيَّتِهِ.

[٧] وأن لا يَعتَقِدَ فَرْضًا مِن فُروضِهِ سُنَّةً.

[٨] وَالماءُ الطَّهورُ.

[٩-١٠] وَدُخولُ الوَقتِ وَالمُوالاةُ لِدائِمِ الحَدَثِ.

The prerequisites for ablution are ten:
1. being a Muslim,
2. discernment,
3. being free of menstruation and postnatal bleeding,
4. [being free] of anything that prevents water from reaching the skin;
5. there not being anything on the limbs that would change pure water,
6. knowing its obligatory acts,
7. not believing one of its obligatory acts as being recommended,
8. having purifying water, and

9–10. the time having entered and consecutiveness for someone whose purification is perpetually invalidated.

Purification

Invalidators of Ablution

(فَصلٌ) نَواقِضُ الوُضوءِ أَرْبَعَةُ أَشياءَ:

الأَوَّلُ: الخارجُ مِن أَحَدِ السبيلَينِ - مِن القُبُلِ أَو الدُّبُرِ -، ريحٌ أَو غَيرُهُ إلّا المَنيَّ.

الثّاني: زَوالُ العَقلِ بِنَومٍ أَو غَيرِهِ إلّا قاعِدٍ مُمَكِّنٍ مَقعَدَتَهُ مِنَ الأَرضِ.

الثّالِثُ: اِلتِقاءُ بَشَرَتَي رَجُلٍ وامْرَأَةٍ كَبيرَينِ أَجنَبيَّينِ مِن غَيرِ حائِلٍ.

الرّابعُ: مَسُّ قُبُلِ الآدَميِّ، أَو حَلقَةِ دُبُرِهِ بِبَطنِ الرّاحَةِ، أَو بُطونِ الأَصابِعِ.

The invalidators of ablution are four things.

The first is whatever exits from either of the two waste passages: front or back, gas or otherwise – except for ejaculate.

The second is the loss of consciousness through sleep or otherwise – except the sleep of someone whose buttocks are firmly seated on the ground.

The third is direct skin contact between male and female adults.

The fourth is touching a human's genitals or anus with the underside of the hand [i.e., the palm] or fingers.

Things Unlawful Due to Impurification
Due to Invalidated Ablution

(فَصْلٌ) مَنِ انْتَقَضَ وُضوءُهُ حَرُمَ عَلَيهِ أَرْبَعَةُ أَشْياءَ:

[١] الصَّلاةُ.

[٢] والطَّوافُ.

[٣] ومَسُّ المُصحَفِ.

[٤] وحَمْلُهُ.

The things unlawful to someone whose ablution is invalidated are four:
1. prayer,
2. circumambulating [the Ka'bah],
3–4. touching and carrying the written Quran [*muṣḥaf*].

Due to Sexual Impurification

وَيَحرُمُ على الجُنُبِ سِتَّةُ أَشياءَ:

[١] الصَّلاةُ.

[٢] والطَّوافُ.

[٣] ومَسُّ المُصحَفِ.

[٤] وحَمْلُهُ.

[٥] واللَّبْثُ في المَسجِدِ.

[٦] وقِراءَةُ القُرآنِ بِقَصدِ القِراءَةِ.

Purification

The things unlawful to someone with sexual impurity [*junub*] are six:
1. prayer,
2. circumambulating [the Ka'bah],
3–4. touching and carrying the written Quran [*muṣḥaf*],
5. remaining in the mosque, and
6. reciting the Quran intending it as recitation.

Due to Menstruation

وَيَحرُمُ بِالحَيضِ عَشَرةُ أَشياءَ:

[١] الصَّلاةُ.

[٢] والطَّوافُ.

[٣] ومَسُّ المُصحَفِ.

[٤] وحَملُهُ.

[٥] واللُّبثُ في المَسجِدِ.

[٦] وقِراءَةُ القُرآنِ.

[٧] والصَّومُ.

[٨] والطَّلاقُ.

[٩] والمُرورُ في المَسجِدِ إِن خافَت تَلويثَهُ.

[١٠] والاسِتِمتاعُ بِما بَينَ السُّرَّةِ والرُّكبَةِ.

The things unlawful during menstruation are ten:
1. prayer,
2. circumambulating [the Ka'bah],

3–4. touching and carrying the written Quran [*muṣḥaf*],
5. remaining in the mosque,
6. reciting Quran,
7. fasting,
8. divorce,
9. passing through the mosque if one fears to soil it, and
10. sexual enjoyment in the area [of the body] between the navel and the knees.

Dry Ablution
Causes

$$\text{(فَصْلٌ) أَسْبَابُ التَّيَمُّمِ ثَلَاثَةٌ:}$$
$$\text{[١] فَقْدُ الماءِ.}$$
$$\text{[٢] والْمَرَضُ.}$$
$$\text{[٣] والاحتياجُ إليهِ لِعَطَشِ حَيَوانٍ مُحتَرَمٍ.}$$

The causes of dry ablution [*tayamum*] are three:
1. lack of water,
2. sickness, and
3. needing it to slake the thirst of an honorable living being.

$$\text{غَيرُ الْمُحتَرَمِ سِتَّةٌ:}$$
$$\text{[١] تارِكُ الصَّلاةِ.}$$
$$\text{[٢] والزَّاني الْمُحصَنُ.}$$
$$\text{[٣] والْمُرتَدُّ.}$$

Purification

[٤] والكافِرُ الحَربيُّ.

[٥] والكَلبُ العَقورُ.

[٦] والخِنزيرُ.

Dishonorable living beings are six:
1. those who have abandoned prayer,
2. fornicators with the means to remain chaste,
3. apostates,
4. disbelievers at war with Islam,
5. vicious dogs, and
7. pigs.

Conditions

(فَصلٌ) شُروطُ التَّيَمُّمِ عَشَرَةٌ:

[١] أَن يَكونَ بِتُرابٍ.

[٢] وأن يَكونَ التُّرابُ طاهِرًا.

[٣] وأن لا يَكونَ مُستَعمَلًا.

[٤] وأن لا يُخالِطَهُ دَقيقٌ ونَحوُهُ.

[٥] وأن يَقصِدَهُ.

[٦] وأن يَمسَحَ وجهَهُ ويَدَيهِ بِضَربَتَينِ.

[٧] وأن يُزيلَ النَّجاسَةَ أَوَّلًا.

[٨] وأن يَجتَهِدَ في القِبلَةِ قَبلَهُ.

[٩] وأن يَكونَ التَّيَمُّمُ بَعدَ دُخولِ الوَقتِ.

[١٠] وأن يَتَيَمَّمَ لِكُلِّ فَرضٍ.

The prerequisites for dry ablutions are ten:
1. it is performed with soil;
3–4. the soil be pure, unused, and not mixed with flour or the like;
5. its use is deliberate;
6. one wipes his hands and face using two strikes;
7. one removes filth beforehand;
8. ones strive to determine the direction of prayer beforehand;
9. its performance occurs after the time has entered; and
10. one performs dry ablution for each obligation.

Obligatory Actions

(فَصلٌ) فُروضُ التَّيَمُّمِ خَمسَةٌ:

الأَوَّلُ: نَقلُ التُّرابِ.

الثَّاني: النِّيَّةُ.

الثَّالِثُ: مَسحُ الوَجهِ.

الرَّابعُ: مَسحُ اليَدَينِ إِلى المِرفَقَينِ.

الخامِسُ: التَّرتيبُ بَينَ المَسحَتَينِ.

The obligatory actions of dry ablution are five.

The first is transferring the soil.

The second is the intention.

The third is wiping the face.

The fourth is wiping the arms up to [and including] the elbows.

The fifth is the order between the wipes.

Purification

Invalidators

(فَصْلٌ) مُبْطِلاتُ التَّيَمُّمِ ثَلاثَةٌ:

[١] ما أَبْطَلَ الوضوءَ.

[٢] والرِّدَّةَ.

[٣] وتَوَهُّمُ الماءِ إِن تَيَمَّمَ لِفَقْدِهِ.

The invalidators of dry ablution are three:
1. whatever invalidates ablution,
2. apostasy, and
3. imagining [having access to] water if one's dry ablution [was performed] for its lack.

Filth
What Can Be Purified

(فَصْلٌ) الذي يَطْهُرُ مِنَ النَّجاساتِ ثَلاثَةٌ:

[١] الخَمرُ إذا تَخَلَّلَت بِنَفسِها.

[٢] وجِلدُ المَيتَةِ إذا دُبِغَ.

[٣] وما صارَ حَيَواناً.

The types of filth than can be purified are three:
1. wine when it becomes vinegar on its own,
2. the skin of an animal that died without being slaughtered when it is tanned, and
3. whatever becomes a living creature.

Categories

(فَصلٌ) النَّجاساتُ ثَلاثٌ:

[١] مُغَلَّظَةٌ.

[٢] ومُخَفَّفَةٌ.

[٣] ومُتَوَسِّطَةٌ.

المُغَلَّظَةُ: نَجاسَةُ الكَلبِ والخِنزيرِ، وفَرعُ أَحدِهِما.

والمُخَفَّفَةُ: بَولُ الصَّبيِّ الذي لَم يَطعَم غَيرَ اللَّبَنِ، ولَم يَبلُغِ الحَولَينِ.

والمُتَوَسِّطَةُ: سائِرُ النَّجاساتِ.

The [grades of] filth are three:
1. heavy-grade [*mughallaẓah*],
2. light-grade [*mukhaffafah*], and
3. medium-grade [*mutawasaṭah*].

Heavy-grade is the filth of dogs, pigs, and the offspring of either one of them.

Light-grade is urine from a male infant who fed on milk and has not reached two lunar years.

Medium-grade is all other types of filth.

How to Clean

(فَصلٌ) المُغَلَّظَةُ تَطهُرُ بِسَبعِ غَسلاتٍ بَعد إزالَةِ عَينِها إحداهُنَّ بِتُرابٍ.

والمُخَفَّفَةُ تَطهُرُ بِرَشِّ الماءِ عَلَيها مَعَ الغَلَبَةِ وإزالَةِ عَينِها.

والمُتَوَسِّطَةُ تَنقَسِمُ إلىٰ قِسمَينِ: عَينِيَّةٌ وحُكمِيَّةٌ.
العَينِيَّةُ: التي لَها لَونٌ وريحٌ وطَعمٌ؛ فَلا بُدَّ مِن إزالَةِ لَونِها وريحِها وطَعمِها.
والحُكمِيَّةُ: التي لا لَونَ ولا ريحَ ولا طَعمَ لَها، يَكفيكَ جَريُ الماءِ عَلَيها.

Heavy-grade filth is purified through seven washing after having removed its substance, with soil accompanying one of those washings.

Medium-grade filth is purified by dousing it with water provided it overwhelms the affected area, and removes its substance.

Medium-grade filth is divided into two divisions:
1. physical [*'ayniyyah*], and
2. legal [*ḥukmiyyah*].

Physical filth has a color, smell, and taste. Its color, smell, and taste must be removed.

Legal filth is without color, taste, and odor. It is enough that water flows over it.

Menstruation

(فَصلٌ)
أَقَلُّ الحَيضِ: يَومٌ ولَيلَةٌ.
وغالِبُهُ: سِتٌّ أَوِ سَبعٌ.
وأَكثَرُهُ: خَمسَةَ عَشَرَ يَومًا بِلَياليها.

أَقَلُّ الطُّهرِ بَينَ الحَيضَتَينِ: خَمسَةَ عَشَرَ يَومًا.
وغالِبُهُ: أَربَعَةٌ وعِشرونَ يَومًا، أو ثَلاثَةٌ وعِشرونَ يَومًا.
ولا حَدَّ لأكثَرِهِ.
أَقَلُّ النِّفاسِ: مَجَّةٌ.
وغالِبُهُ: أَربَعونَ يَومًا.
وأَكثَرُهُ: سِتُّونَ يَومًا.

The minimal [duration] for menstruation is one day and night. Its typical [length] is six or seven [days]. Its maximum is fifteen days and nights.

The minimal [amount] purification between two menstruations is fifteen days. Its typical [duration] is twenty-four or twenty-three days. There is no limit to its maximum.

The minimal [length of] postnatal bleeding is a moment. Its typical [amount] is forty days. Its maximum is sixty days.

Prayer

Excuses

(فَصلٌ) أعذارُ الصَّلاةِ اثنانِ:

[١] النَّومُ.

[٢] والنِّسيانُ.

The excuses for prayer are two:
1. sleep, and
2. forgetfulness.

Prerequisites

(فَصلٌ) شُروطُ الصَّلاةِ ثَمانيَةٌ:

[١] طَهارَةُ الحَدَثَينِ.

[٢] والطَّهارَةُ عَنِ النَّجاسَةِ في الثَّوبِ والبَدَنِ والمَكانِ.

[٣] وسَترُ العَورَةِ.

[٤] واستِقبالُ القِبلَةِ.

[٥] ودُخولُ الوَقتِ.

[٦] والعِلمُ بِفَرْضِيَّتِها.

[٧] وأَن لا يَعتَقِدَ فَرْضًا مِن فُروضِها سُنَّةً.
[٨] واجتِنابُ المُبطِلاتِ.

The prerequisites for prayer are eight:
1. purity from minor and major impurification;
2. purity of the clothes, body, and place of prayer;
3. covering one's nakedness ['awrah];
4. facing the direction of prayer;
5. the time [for the prayer] having entered;
6. knowing that the prayer is obligatory;
7. not believing ones of its obligatory acts to be recommended; and
8. avoiding invalidators.

Causes of Ritual Impurification

الأَحداثُ اثنانِ:
[١] أَصغَرُ.
[٢] وأَكبَرُ.
فالأَصغَرُ: ما أَوجَبَ الوُضوءَ.
والأَكبَرُ: ما أَوجَبَ الغُسلَ.

The events occasioning purification are two:
1. minor, and
2. major.

Minor events require ablution.

Major events require the purification bath.

Prayer

Categories of Nakedness

العَوراتُ أربَعٌ:
[١] عَورَةُ الرَّجُلِ مُطلَقًا، والأَمَةِ في الصَّلاةِ؛ ما بَينَ السُّرَّةِ والرُّكبَةِ.
[٢] وعَورَةُ الحُرَّةِ في الصَّلاةِ جَميعُ بَدَنِها؛ ما سِوَى الوَجهِ والكَفَّينِ.
[٣] وعَورَةُ الحُرَّةِ والأَمَةِ عِندَ الأَجانِبِ جَميعُ البَدَنِ.
[٤] وعِندَ مَحارِمِهِما والنِّساءِ ما بَينَ السُّرَّةِ والرُّكبَةِ.

The categories of nakedness are four.

1. The nakedness of a man (unconditionally) and of a female slave during prayer is what lies between the navel and the knees.
2. The nakedness of a free woman during prayer is her entire body other than her face and hands.
3. The nakedness of a free female and a slave in front of unrelated men is the entire body.
4. [The nakedness of the last category] when with their male relatives and women is what lies between the navel and the knees.

Performance
Essential Elements

(فَصلٌ) أَركانُ الصَّلاةِ سَبعةَ عَشَرَ:

الأوَّلُ: النِّيَّةُ.

الثَّاني: تَكبيرَةُ الإحرامِ.

الثَّالِثُ: القيامُ علىٰ القادِرِ في الفَرْضِ.

الرَّابعُ: قِراءةُ الفاتِحَةِ.

الخامِسُ: الرُّكوعُ.

السَّادِسُ: الطُّمَأنينَةُ فيهِ.

السَّابعُ: الاعتِدالُ.

الثَّامِنُ: الطُّمَأنينَةُ فيهِ.

التَّاسِعُ: السُّجودُ مَرَّتَينِ.

العاشِرُ: الطُّمَأنينَةُ فيهِ.

الحادي عَشَرَ: الجُلوسُ بَينَ السَّجدَتَينِ.

الثَّاني عَشَرَ: الطُّمَأنينَةُ فيهِ.

الثَّالِثَ عَشَرَ: التَّشَهُّدُ الأَخيرُ.

الرَّابعَ عَشَرَ: القُعودُ فيهِ.

الخامِسَ عَشَرَ: الصَّلاةُ علىٰ النَّبيِّ ﷺ فيهِ.

Prayer

السَّادِسَ عَشَرَ: السَّلامُ.

السَّابَعَ عَشَرَ: التَّرتيبُ.

The essential elements of prayer are seventeen.

The first is the intention.

The second is the inaugural saying of "*Allāhu akbar.*"

The third is standing for those able to do so – in obligatory prayers.

The fourth is reciting Al-Fātiḥah.

The fifth is bowing.

The sixth is reposing therein.

The seventh is rising.

The eighth is reposing therein.

The ninth is prostrating twice.

The tenth is reposing therein.

The eleventh is sitting between the two prostrations.

The twelfth is reposing therein.

The thirteenth is the final *tashahhud*.

The fourteenth is sitting for it.

The fifteenth is praying upon the Prophet (may Allah bless him and give him peace).

The sixteenth is saying "*As-salāmu 'alaykum.*"

The seventeenth is the order.

Intention

(فَصلٌ) النِّيَّةُ ثَلاثُ دَرَجاتٍ:

[١] إنْ كانَتِ الصَّلاةُ فَرْضًا، وَجَبَ قَصدُ الفِعلِ والتَّعيينُ والفَرْضيَّةُ.

[٢] وإن كانَت نافِلَةً مُؤَقَّتَةً؛ كَراتِبَةٍ أو ذاتِ سَبَبٍ، وَجَبَ قَصدُ الفِعلِ والتَّعيينُ.

[٣] وإن كانَت نافِلَةً مُطلَقَةً وَجَبَ قَصدُ الفِعلِ فَقَط.

Intentions are of three grades.

1. If the prayer is obligatory, it is obligatory that one deliberates to perform the action, identify it, and [intends it] as an obligation.
2. If it is recommended for a specific time (like the recommended prayers associated with obligatory prayers [*rātibah*]) or it has a cause, it is obligatory that one deliberates to perform the action and identifies it.
3. If it is purely voluntary, it is only obligatory that one deliberates to perform the action.

الفِعلُ: «أُصَلِّي».

والتَّعيينُ: «ظُهرًا» أو «عَصرًا».

والفَرْضيَّةُ: «فَرْضًا».

The action is: "I pray."

Identifying it is: "Noon Prayer" or "Midafternoon Prayer."

Its being obligatory: "as an obligation."

The Prerequisites for The Inaugural "Allāhu Akbar"

(فَصلٌ) شُروطُ تَكبيرَةِ الإحرامِ سِتَّةَ عَشَرَ:

[١] أَن تَقَعَ حالَةَ القيامِ في الفَرْضِ.

Prayer

[٢] وأَن تكونَ بالعَرَبيَّةِ.

[٣-٤] وأَن تكونَ بِلَفظِ الجَلالةِ وبِلَفظِ «أكبَرُ».

[٥] والتَّرتيبُ بَينَ اللَّفظَينِ.

[٦] وأَن لا يَمُدَّ هَمزَةَ «الجَلالةِ».

[٧] وعَدَمُ مَدِّ باءِ «أكبَرُ».

[٨] وأَن لا يُشَدِّدَ «الباءَ».

[٩] وأَن لا يَزيدَ واوًا ساكِنةً أو مُتَحَرِّكةً بَينَ الكَلِمَتَينِ.

[١٠] وأَن لا يَزيدَ واوًا قَبلَ الجَلالةِ.

[١١] وأَن لا يَقِفَ بَينَ كَلِمَتَي التَّكبيرِ وَقفَةً طَويلَةً ولا قَصيرَةً.

[١٢] وأَن يُسمِعَ نَفسَهُ جَميعَ حُروفِها.

[١٣] ودُخولُ الوَقتِ في المُؤَقَّتِ.

[١٤] وإيقاعُها حالَ الاستِقبالِ.

[١٥] وأَن لا يُخِلَّ بِحَرفٍ مِن حُروفِها.

[١٦] وتَأخيرُ تَكبيرَةِ المَأمومِ عَن تَكبيرَةِ الإمامِ.

The conditions for the inaugural saying of "*Allāhu akbar*" are sixteen.

1. That it occurs while standing (for obligatory prayers);
2. it is in Arabic;
3. it uses the phrase "*Allāh*";
4. it uses the phrase "*Akbar*";
5. the two phrases are in order;

6. not elongating the [initial] *hamzah* of "*Allāh*";
7. not elongating the *bā'* in "*Akbar*";
8. not doubling the *bā'*;
9. not adding a *wāw* (with or without a vowel) before "*Allāh*";
10. not adding a *wāw* before "*Allāh*";
11. not pausing between the two words of the inaugural saying of "*Allāhu akbar*" – neither a long nor short pause;
12. making all of its letters audible to himself;
13. the time having entered – for a prayer with a set time;
14. its [utterance] taking place while facing [the direction of prayer];
15. not voiding one of its letters; and
16. the follower's saying of it occurring after the imam's.

Preconditions for Al-Fātiḥah

(فَصلٌ) شُروطُ الفاتِحَةِ عَشَرَةٌ:

[١] التَّرتيبُ.

[٢] والمُوالاةُ.

[٣] ومُراعاةُ حُروفِها.

[٤] ومُراعاةُ تَشديداتِها.

[٥] وأَن لا يَسكُتَ سَكتَةً طَويلَةً ولا قَصيرَةً يَقصِدُ بِها قَطعَ القِراءَةِ.

Prayer

[٦] وقِراءَةُ كُلِّ آياتِها، ومِنها البَسمَلَةُ.
[٧] وعَدَمُ اللَّحنِ المُخِلِّ بِالمَعنَى.
[٨] وأَن تَكونَ حالَةَ القِيامِ في الفَرْضِ.
[٩] وأَن يُسمِعَ نَفسَهُ القِراءَةَ.
[١٠] وأَن لا يَتَخَلَّلَها ذِكرٌ أَجنَبِيٌّ.

The prerequisites of [reciting] Al-Fātiḥah are ten:
1. the order,
2. the consecutiveness,
3–4. observing its letters and doubled letters,
5. not making a silent pause, nor a short pause with the intent of interrupting the recitation,
6. reciting all of its verses (which include saying "*Bismi Llāhi r-raḥmāni r-raḥīm*"),
7. not mispronouncing it in a way that voids its meaning,
8. it occurring while one is standing (in obligatory prayers),
9. making the recitation audible to oneself, and
10. it not being interrupted by unrelated remembrance.

Al-Fātiḥah's Doubled Letters

(فَصلٌ) تَشديداتُ الفاتِحَةِ أَربَعَ عَشَرَةَ:
[١] ﴿بِسمِ اللَّهِ﴾ فَوقَ اللامِ.
[٢] ﴿الرَّحمنِ﴾ فَوقَ الرَّاءِ.
[٣] ﴿الرَّحيمِ﴾ فَوقَ الرَّاءِ.

[٤] ﴿الحَمدُ لِلَّهِ﴾ فَوقَ لامِ الجَلالَةِ.

[٥] ﴿رَبِّ العالَمينَ﴾ فَوقَ الباءِ.

[٦] ﴿الرَّحمنِ﴾ فَوقَ الرَّاءِ.

[٧] ﴿الرَّحيمِ﴾ فَوقَ الرَّاءِ.

[٨] ﴿مالِكِ يَومِ الدِّينِ﴾ فَوقَ الدَّالِ.

[٩] ﴿إِيَّاكَ نَعبُدُ﴾ فَوقَ الياءِ.

[١٠] ﴿إِيَّاكَ نَستَعينُ﴾ فَوقَ الياءِ.

[١١] ﴿اهدِنا الصِّراطَ المُستَقيمَ﴾ فَوقَ الصَّادِ.

[١٢] ﴿صِراطَ الَّذينَ﴾ فَوقَ اللّامِ.

[١٣، ١٤] ﴿أَنعَمتَ عَلَيهِم غَيرِ المَغضوبِ عَلَيهِم وَلا الضَّالِّينَ﴾ فَوقَ الضَّادِ واللّامِ.

The doubled letters of Al-Fātiḥah are fourteen:
1. "*bismi Llāhi*" – above the *lām*,
2. "*ar-raḥmān*" – above the *rāʾ*,
3. "*ar-raḥīm*" – above the *rāʾ*,
4. "*al-ḥamdu li-Llāhī*" – above the lām of "*Allāh*,"
5. "*rabbu l-ʿālamīn*" – above the *bāʾ*,
6. "*ar-raḥmān*" – above the *rāʾ*,
7. "*ar-raḥīm*" – above the *rāʾ*,
8. "*māliki yaumi d-dīn*" – above the *dāl*,
9. "*iyyāka naʿbudu*" – above the *yāʾ*,
10. "*iyyāka nastaʿīn*" – above the *yāʾ*,
11. "*ihdina ṣ-ṣirāṭ al-mustaqīn*" – above the *ṣād*,
12. "*ṣirāṭa l-ladhīna*" – above the *lām*,

Prayer

13–14. *"an'amta 'alayhim, ghayri l-maghḍūbi 'alayhim, wa la ḍ-ḍāllīn"* – above the *ḍād* and the *lām*.

Raising The Hands

(فَصْلٌ) يُسَنُّ رَفعُ اليَدَينِ في أربَعَةِ مَواضِعَ:
[١] عِندَ تَكبيرَةِ الإحرامِ.
[٢] وعِندَ الرُّكوعِ.
[٣] وعِندَ الاعتِدالِ.
[٤] وعِندَ القيامِ مِن التَّشَهُّدِ الأَوَّلِ.

It is recommended to raise the hands in four places:
1. when [saying] the inaugural *"Allāhu akbar,"*
2. when bowing,
3. when rising, and
4. when standing from the first *tashahhud*.

The Preconditions for Prostrating

(فَصْلٌ) شُروطُ السُّجودِ سَبعَةٌ:
[١] أَن يَسجُدَ علىٰ سَبعَةِ أَعضاءٍ.
[٢] وأن تَكونَ جَبهَتُهُ مَكشوفَةٍ.
[٣] والتَّحامُلُ بِرَأسِهِ.
[٤] وعَدَمُ الهُويِّ لِغَيرِهِ.
[٥] وأن لا يَسجُدَ علىٰ شَيءٍ يَتَحَرَّكُ بِحَرَكَتِهِ.

[٦] وَارتِفاعُ أَسافِلِهِ علىٰ أَعالِيهِ.
[٧] والطُّمَأْنِينَةُ فيهِ.

The preconditions for prostrating are seven:
1. prostrating upon the seven limbs,
2. the forehead being bare,
3. his head bearing [some of his] weight,
4. not descending for any other reason,
5. not prostrating upon something that moves with his movements,
6. his posterior being higher than his upper body, and
7. reposing therein.

Limbs of Prostration

(خاتِمَةٌ) أَعضاءُ السُّجودِ سَبعَةٌ:
[١] الجَبهَةُ.
[٢-٣] وبُطونُ أَصابِعِ الكَفَّينِ.
[٤-٥] والرُّكبَتانِ.
[٦-٧] وبُطونُ أَصابِعِ الرِّجلَينِ.

(Closing) The limbs of prostration are seven:
1. the forehead,
2–3. the two palms,
4–5. the two knees, and
6–7. the bottoms of the fingers and toes.

Prayer

The Tashahhud's Doubled Letters

(فَصلٌ) تَشديداتُ التَّشَهُّدِ إِحدَىٰ وعِشرونَ؛ خَمسٌ [زائِدَةٌ] في أَكمَلِهِ، وسِتَّ عَشرَةَ في أَقَلِّهِ:

[١-٢] «التَّحيَّاتُ» علىٰ التَّاءِ والياءِ.

[٣] «المُبارَكاتُ الصَّلَواتُ» علىٰ الصادِ.

[٤-٥] و«الطَّيِّباتُ» علىٰ الطَّاءِ والياءِ.

[٦] «لِلّٰهِ» علىٰ لامِ الجَلالَةِ.

[٧] «السَّلامُ» علىٰ السّينِ.

[٨-١٠] «عَلَيكَ أَيُّها النَّبيُّ» علىٰ الياءِ والنُّونِ والياءِ.

[١١] «ورَحمَةُ اللَّهِ» علىٰ لامِ الجَلالَةِ.

[١٢] «وبَرَكاتُهُ السَّلامُ» علىٰ السّينِ.

[١٣] «عَلَينا وعلىٰ عِبادِ اللَّهِ» علىٰ لامِ الجَلالةِ.

[١٤] «الصَّالِحينَ» علىٰ الصادِ.

[١٥] «أَشهَدُ أَن لَّا إِلَهَ» علىٰ لامِ أَلِفٍ.

[١٦-١٧] و«إلَّا اللَّهُ» علىٰ لامِ أَلِفٍ ولامِ الجَلالَةِ.

[١٨] «وأَشهَدُ أَنَّ» علىٰ النُّونِ.

[١٩-٢١] و«مُحَمَّدًا رَّسولُ اللَّهِ».. علىٰ ميمِ مُحَمَّدٍ، وعلىٰ الرَّاءِ، وعلىٰ لامِ الجَلالَةِ.

The doubled letters in the *tashahhud* are twenty-one: five [extras] in its complete form, sixteen in its minimal form:

1–2. "*at-taḥiyyāt*" – on the *tā'* and the *yā'*;
3. "*al-mubārakāt aṣ-ṣalawāt*" – on the *ṣād*;
4–5. "*aṭ-ṭayyibāt*" – on the *ṭā'* and *yā'*;
6. "*li-Llāh*" on the *lām*;
7. "*as-salām*" – on the *sīn*;
8–10. "*'alayka ayyuha n-nabiyy*" – on the *yā'* and *nūn* and *yā'*;
11. "*wa raḥmatu Llāhi*" – on the *lām*;
12. "*wa barakātuhu, as-salāmu*" – on the *sīn*;
13. "*'alaynā wa 'alā 'ibādi Llāhi*" – on the *lām* of "*Allāh*";
14. "*aṣ-ṣāliḥīn*" – on the *ṣād*;
15. "*ashhadu al-lā ilāha*" – on the *lām alif*;
16–17. "*illā Llāh*" – on the *lām alif* and *lām* of "*Allāh*";
18. "*wa ashhadu ann*" – on the *nūn*;
19–20. "*Muḥammadan rasūli l-Lāh*" – on the *mīm* of "*Muḥammad*," and the *rā'*, and
21. the *lām* of "*Allāh*".

Supplicating upon The Prophet ﷺ: Doubled Letters

(فَصلٌ) تَشديداتُ أَقَلِّ الصَّلاةِ علىٰ النَّبيِّ أَرَبَعٌ:

[١] «اللَّهُمَّ» علىٰ اللَّامِ والميمِ.

[٢] «صَلِّ» علىٰ اللَّامِ.

[٣] «علىٰ مُحَمَّدٍ» علىٰ الميمِ.

The doubled letters in the minimal supplication upon the Prophet (may Allah bless him and give him peace) are four:

1–2. "*Allāhumma*" – on the *lām* and *mīm*,
3. "*ṣalli*" – on the *lām*, and
4. "*ʿalā Muḥammad*" – on the *mīm*.

Minimum "As-Salāmu ʿAlaykum"

(فَصلٌ) أَقَلُّ السَّلامِ: «السَّلامُ عَلَيكُم»، تشديدُ «السَّلامُ» عَلى السّينِ.

The minimal [closing] saying of "*As-salāmu ʿalaykum*" is "*As-salāmu ʿalaykum*" – with its *sīn* doubled.

Prayer Times

(فَصلٌ) أوقاتِ الصَّلاةِ خَمسَةٌ:

[١] أَوَّلُ وَقتِ الظُّهرِ زَوالُ الشَّمسِ، وآخِرُهُ مَصيرُ ظِلِّ الشيءِ مِثلَهُ؛ غَيرَ ظِلِّ الاستِواءِ.

[٢] وأَوَّلُ وَقتِ العَصرِ إذا صارَ ظِلُّ كُلِّ شَيءٍ مِثلَهُ، وزادَ قَليلًا، وآخِرُهُ عِندَ غُروبُ الشَّمسِ.

[٣] وأَوَّلُ وَقتِ المَغرِبِ غُروبُ الشَّمسِ، وآخِرُهُ غُروبُ الشَّفَقِ الأَحمَرِ.

[٤] وأَوَّلُ وَقتِ العِشاءِ غُروبُ الشَّفَقِ الأَحمَرِ، وآخِرُهُ طُلوعُ الفَجرِ الصّادِقِ.

[٥] وأَوَّلُ وَقتِ الصُّبحِ طُلوعُ الفَجرِ الصّادِقِ، وأَخِرُهُ طُلوعُ الشَّمسِ.

The times for prayer are five.
1. The beginning of the time for Noon Prayer is when the sun passes the zenith; its end is when an object's shadow equals itself discounting its shadow at the zenith.
2. The beginning for Midafternoon Prayer is when an object's shadow equals itself plus a little more; its end is [at] sunset.
3. The beginning for Sunset Prayer is [at] sunset; its end is [at] the disappearance of the red glow.
4. The beginning for Night Prayer is [at] the disappearance of the red glow; its end is [at] true dawn.
5. The beginning for Morning Prayer is true dawn; its end is [at] sunrise.

الأَشفاقُ ثَلاثَةٌ:

[١] أَحمَرُ.

[٢] وأَصفَرُ.

[٣] وأَبيَضُ.

الأَحمَرُ مَغرِبٌ.

وَالأَصفَرُ والأَبيَضُ عِشاءٌ.

وَيُندَبُ تَأخيرُ صَلاةِ العِشاءِ إلىٰ أن يَغيبَ الشَّفَقُ الأَصفَرُ والأَبيَضُ.

The glows along the horizon are three:
1. red,
2. yellow, and
3. white.

Prayer

The red is sunset.

The yellow and white are nightfall.

It is recommended to delay Night Prayer until the yellow and white glows disappear.

Times When It Is Unlawful To Pray

(فَصلٌ) تَحرُمُ الصَّلاةُ التي لَيسَ لَها سَبَبٌ مُتَقَدِّمٌ ولا مُقارِنٌ في خَمسَةِ أوقاتٍ:

[١] عِندَ طُلوعِ الشَّمسِ حتَّىٰ تَرتَفِعَ قَدرَ رُمحٍ.

[٢] وعِندَ الإستِواءِ في غيرِ يَومِ الجُمُعَةِ حتَّىٰ تَزولَ.

[٣] وعِندَ الإصفِرارِ حتَّىٰ تَغرُبَ.

[٤] وبَعدَ صَلاةِ الصُّبحِ حتَّىٰ تَطلُعَ.

[٥] وبَعدَ صَلاةِ العَصرِ حتَّىٰ تَغرُبَ.

Prayers that are not occasioned by a cause that is prior or concurrent [to the prayer] are unlawful during five times:

1. when the sun rises until it has risen the amount of a spear,
2. when the sun is at its highest point (except on Friday) until it begins to descend,
3. when the sun yellows until it sets,
4. after Morning Prayer until the sun rises, and
5. after Midafternoon Prayer until sunset.

Pauses for Silence

(فَصلٌ) سَكتاتُ الصَّلاةِ سِتٌّ:

[١] بَينَ تَكبيرَةِ الإحرامِ ودُعاءِ الافتِتاحِ.

[٢] وبَينَ دُعاءِ الافتِتاحِ والتَّعَوُّذِ.

[٣] وبَينَ الفاتِحَةِ والتَّعَوُّذِ.

[٤] وبَينَ آخِرِ الفاتِحَةِ وآمينَ.

[٥] وبَينَ آمينَ والسُّورَةِ.

[٦] وبَينَ السُّورَةِ والرُّكوعِ.

The pauses for silence during prayer are six:
1. Between the inaugural "*Allāhu akbar*" and the opening supplication,
2. [between the opening supplication and] the seeking of protecting,
3. between Al-Fātiḥah and the seeking of protection,
4. between the end of Al-Fātiḥah and saying "*Āmīn*,"
5. between "*Āmīn*" and the surah, and
6. between the surah and bowing.

Elements Requiring Reposing

(فَصلٌ) الأركانُ التي تَلزَمُ فيها الطُّمَأنينَةُ أَربَعَةٌ:

[١] الرُّكوعُ.

[٢] والاعتِدالُ.

[٣] والسُّجودُ.

[٤] والجُلوسُ بَينَ السَّجدَتَينِ.
الطُّمَأنينَةُ هيَ: سُكونٌ بَعدَ حَرَكَةٍ؛ بِحَيثُ يَستَقِرُّ كُلُّ عُضوٍ مَحَلَّهُ بِقَدرِ «سُبحانَ اللَّهِ».

The essential elements wherein reposing is required are four:
1. bowing,
2. standing from it,
3. prostrating, and
4. sitting between the prostrations.

Reposing is to become motionless after being in motion in a manner that all limbs rest in their place long enough to say "*Subḥān Allāh.*"

Causes of The Prostration of Forgetfulness

(فَصلٌ) أسبابُ سُجودِ السَّهوِ أربَعَةٌ:
الأوَّلُ: تَركُ بَعضٍ مِن أبعاضِ الصَّلاةِ، أو بَعضِ البَعضِ.
الثَّاني: فِعلُ ما يُبطِلُ عَمدُهُ، ولا يُبطِلُ سَهوُهُ؛ إذا فَعَلَهُ ناسِيًا.
الثَّالِثُ: نَقلُ رُكنٍ قَوليٍّ إلى غَيرِ مَحَلِّهِ.
الرَّابعُ: إيقاعُ رُكنٍ فِعليٍّ مَع احتِمالِ الزِّيادَةِ.

The causes of the prostration for forgetfulness are four.

The first is omitting one of the greater recommended acts [*abʿāḍ*] of prayer – or one of their parts.

The second is performing whose deliberate performance invalidates the prayer, but when whose absent-minded for forced performance does not.

The third is moving an essential utterance from its [proper] place.

The fourth is performing an essential act that may be superfluous.

The Greater Recommended Acts

(فَصلٌ) أبعاضُ الصَّلاةِ سَبعَةٌ:

[١] التَّشَهُّدُ الأوَّلُ.

[٢] وقُعودُهُ.

[٣] والصَّلاةُ علىٰ النَّبيِّ ﷺ فيهِ.

[٤] والصَّلاةُ علىٰ الآلِ في التَّشَهُّدِ الأخيرِ.

[٥] والقُنوتُ.

[٦] وقِيامُهُ.

[٧] والصَّلاةُ والسَّلامُ علىٰ النَّبيِّ ﷺ وآلِهِ وصَحبِهِ فيهِ.

The greater recommended acts [ab'āḍ] of prayer are seven:

1. the first *tashahhud*,
2. sitting for it,
3. supplicating upon the Prophet (may Allah bless him and give him peace) during it,
4. supplicating upon the household during the final *tashahhud*;
5-6. the Qunūt Supplication and standing for it, and
7. supplicating upon the Prophet (may Allah bless him and give him peace) and his household therein.

Prayer

Prayer Invalidators

(فَصلٌ) تَبطُلُ الصَّلاةُ بِأَربَعَ عَشرَةَ خَصلَةً:

[١] بِالحَدَثِ.

[٢] وبِوُقوعِ النَّجاسَةِ إن لَم تُلقَ حالًا مِن غَيرِ حَملٍ.

[٣] وانكِشافِ العَورَةِ إن لَم تُستَر حالًا.

[٤] والنُّطقِ بِحَرفَينِ أو حَرفٍ مُفهِمٍ عَمدًا.

[٥] وبِالمُفَطِّرِ عَمدًا.

[٦] وبِالأُكلِ الكَثيرِ ناسِيًا.

[٧] وثَلاثِ حَرَكاتٍ مُتَوالِياتٍ ولَو سَهوًا.

[٨] والوَثبَةِ الفاحِشَةِ.

[٩] والضَّربَةِ المُفرِطَةِ.

[١٠] وزِيادَةِ رُكنٍ فِعلِيٍّ عَمدًا.

[١١] والتَّقَدُّمِ علىٰ إمامِهِ بِرُكنَينِ والتخَلُّفِ بِهِما بِغَيرِ عُذرٍ.

[١٢] ونِيَّةِ قَطعِ الصَّلاةِ.

[١٣] وتَعليقِ قَطعِها بِشيءٍ.

[١٤] والتَّرَدُّدِ في قَطعِها.

Prayer is invalidated through fourteen things:
1. the occurrence of what occasions impurification;
2. the presence of filth if it is not cast off without holding it;

3. the exposure of one's nakedness if it is not covered immediately;
4. uttering two letters or one that conveys meaning – deliberately;
5. the occurrence of something whose deliberate performance breaks one's fast;
6. forgetfully eating a large amount;
7. three consecutive motions – even absentmindedly;
8. a broad jump;
9. excessively striking [with the hand];
10. deliberately adding an additional essential action;
11. preceding one's imam by two essential actions, and inexcusably lagging behind the imam by two essential actions;
12. intending to interrupt prayer;
13. making its interruption conditional upon an event; and
14. indecision about interrupting it.

Congregational Prayer
Conditions For Leading

(فَصلٌ) الذي يَلزَمُ فيهِ نيَّةُ الإمامَةِ أَربَعٌ:

[١] الجُمُعَةُ.

[٢] والمُعادَةُ.

[٣] والمَنذورَةُ جَماعَةً.

[٤] والمُتَقَدِّمَةُ في المَطَرِ.

Prayer

[The prayers] that require the intention to lead [others] are four:
1. Friday Prayer,
2. carrying out a repeat performance,
3. carrying out a prayer one has vowed to pray in congregation, and
4. the first prayer when [joining due to] rain.

Conditions for Following

(فَصلٌ) شُروطُ القُدوَةِ أَحَدَ عَشَرَ:

[١] أَن لا يَعلَمَ بُطلانَ صَلاةِ إمامِهِ بِحَدَثٍ أو غَيرِهِ.

[٢] وأَن لا يَعتَقِدَ وُجوبَ قَضائِها عَلَيهِ.

[٣] وأَن لا يَكونَ مَأمومًا.

[٤] ولا أُمِّيًّا.

[٥] وأَن لا يَتَقَدَّمَ علىٰ إمامِهِ في المَوقِفِ.

[٦] وأَن يَعلَمَ انتِقالاتِ إمامِهِ.

[٧] وأَن يَجتَمِعا في مَسجِدٍ، أو في ثَلاثِ مِئَةِ ذِراعٍ تَقريبًا.

[٨] وأَن يَنويَ القُدوَةَ أو الجَماعَةَ.

[٩] وأَن يَتَوافَقَ نَظمُ صَلاتَيهِما.

[١٠] وأَن لا يُخالِفَهُ في سُنَّةٍ فاحِشَةِ المُخالَفَةِ.

[١١] وأَن يُتابِعَهْ.

The conditions for following [an imam] are eleven:
1. not knowing that the imam's prayer has been invalidated by what occasions the need for ritual purification [ḥadath] or something else;
2. not believing that one will be obligated to repeat the prayer;
3. that he [the imam] is not being led;
4. not being illiterate [in reciting Al-Fātiḥah];
5. not standing in front of him;
6. knowing the imam's transitions [from position to position];
7. them being together in a mosque or within, approximately, 300 *dhirā*'s [144 meters, 472 feet];
8. intending to follow or to pray with a congregation;
9. their two prayers matching in their outward organization;
10. not diverging from the imam in a sunnah that is [considered to be] a significant divergence; and
11. following him.

Forms of Leading And Following

(فَصْلٌ) صُوَرُ القُدوَةِ تِسعٌ:
تَصِحُّ في خَمسٍ:
[١] قُدوَةُ رَجُلٍ بِرَجُلٍ.
[٢] وقُدوَةُ امرَأَةٍ بِرَجُلٍ.
[٣] وقُدوَةُ خُنثىٰ بِرَجُلٍ.

Prayer

[٤] وقُدوَةُ امرَأةٍ بِخُنثىٰ.

[٥] وقُدوَةُ امرَأةٍ بامرَأةٍ.

The scenarios for following [an imam] are nine. Following is valid in five [scenarios]:
1. a man following a man,
2. a woman following a man,
3. a hermaphrodite [*khunthā*] following a man,
4. a woman following a hermaphrodite, and
5. a woman following a woman.

وَتَبطُلُ في أَربَعٍ:

[١] قُدوَةُ رَجُلٍ بامرَأةٍ.

[٢] وقُدوَةُ رَجُلٍ بِخُنثىٰ.

[٣] وقُدوَةُ خُنثىٰ بامرَأةٍ.

[٤] وقُدوَةُ خُنثىٰ بِخُنثىٰ.

It is invalid in four [scenarios]:
1. a man following a woman;
2. a man following a hermaphrodite;
3. a hermaphrodite following a woman; and
4. a hermaphrodite following a hermaphrodite.

Shortening And Joining Prayers
The Conditions For Preemptive Joining

(فصلٌ) شُروطُ جَمعِ التقديمِ أَربَعةٌ:

[١] البَداءَةُ بالأُولىٰ.

[٢] ونيَّةُ الجَمعِ فيها.

[٣] والمُوالاةُ بَيْنَهُما.

[٤] ودَوامُ العُذرِ.

The conditions for preemptive joining are four:
1. beginning with the first [prayer],
2. the intention to join during its performance,
3. consecutiveness between the two [prayers], and
4. the excuse continuing.

The Conditions for Delayed Joining

(فَصلٌ) شُروطُ جَمعِ التأخيرِ اثنانِ:

[١] نيَّةُ التَّأخيرِ وقَد بَقِيَ مِن وَقتِ الأُولىٰ ما يَسَعُها.

[٢] ودَوامُ العَذرِ إلىٰ تَمامِ الثَّانيَةِ.

The conditions for delayed joining are two:
1. the intention to delay occurring while there is still enough time remaining for the first prayer to have prayed it, and
2. the excuse [for joining] continuing until finishing the second [prayer].

The Conditions for Shortening

(فَصلٌ) شُروطُ القَصرِ سَبعَةٌ:

[١] أَن يَكونَ سَفَرُهُ مَرحَلَتَينِ.

[٢] وأَن يَكونَ مُباحًا.

[٣] والعِلمُ بِجَوازِ القَصرِ.

Prayer

[٤] وَنِيَّةُ القَصرِ عِندَ الإحرامِ.
[٥] وَأَن تَكونَ الصَّلاةُ رُباعِيَّةً.
[٦] وَدَوامُ السَّفَرِ إلىٰ تَمامِها.
[٧] وَأَن لا يَقتَدِيَ بِمُتِمٍّ في جُزءٍ مِن صَلاتِهِ.

The conditions for shortening are seven:
1. his journey lasting [at least] two *marḥalah*s [approximately 81 kilometers or 50 miles],
2. the journey being permissible,
3. knowing that shortening is permissible,
4. the intention to shorten during the inaugural "*Allāhu akbar*,"
5. the prayer being a four prayer-cycle prayer;
6. the journey continuing throughout the prayer's completion; and
7. no part of one's prayer is prayed while following someone who is praying in full.

Friday Prayer
Conditions for The Friday Prayer

(فَصلٌ) شُروطُ الجُمُعَةِ سِتَّةٌ:
[١] أَن تَكونَ كُلُّها في وَقتِ الظُّهرِ.
[٢] وَأَن تُقامَ في خُطَّةِ البَلَدِ.
[٣] وَأَن تُصَلَّىٰ جَماعَةً.
[٤] وَأَن يَكونوا أَربَعينَ؛ أَحرارًا، ذُكورًا، بالِغينَ، مُستَوطِنينَ.

Ark of Salvation

[٥] وأَن لا تَسبِقَها ولا تُقارِنَها جُمُعَةٌ في ذلكَ البَلَدِ.

[٦] وأَن يَتَقَدَّمَها خُطبَتانِ.

The conditions for Friday Prayer are six:
1. its entire performance occurs during the time for Noon Prayer,
2. it is held within the municipality's boundaries,
3-4. it is performed as a congregation numbering forty free adult males who are permanent residents,
5. its performance not be preceded or concurrent to another Friday prayer in the same municipality, and
6. it is preceded by two sermons.

Essential Elements of The Sermons

(فَصلٌ) أركانُ الخُطبَتَينِ خَمسَةٌ:

[١] حَمدُ اللَّهِ فيهِما.

[٢] والصَّلاةُ على النَّبيِّ ﷺ فيهِما.

[٣] والوَصيَّةُ بِالتَّقوى فيهِما.

[٤] وقِراءَةُ آيَةٍ مِنَ القُرآنِ في إحداهُما.

[٥] والدُّعاءُ لِلمُؤمِنينَ والمُؤمِناتِ في الأَخيرَةِ.

The essential elements of the two sermons are five:
1. praising Allah in them both,
2. supplications upon the Prophet (may Allah bless him and give him peace) in them both,
3. advising being mindful of Allah in them both,

4. reciting a verse of the Quran in one of them, and
5. supplicating for male and female believers in the second.

Prerequisites for The Sermons

(فَصلٌ) شُروطُ الخُطبَتَينِ عَشَرَةٌ:

[١] الطَّهارَةُ عَنِ الحَدَثَينِ الأَصغَرِ والأَكبَرِ.

[٢] والطَّهارَةُ عَنِ النَّجاسِةِ في الثَّوبِ والبَدَنِ والمَكانِ.

[٣] وسَترُ العَورَةِ.

[٤] والقيامُ علىٰ القادِرِ.

[٥] والجُلوسُ بَينَهُما فَوقَ طُمَأنينَةِ الصَّلاةِ.

[٦] والمُوالاةُ بَينَهُما.

[٧] والمُوالاةُ بَينَهُما وبَينَ الصَّلاةِ.

[٨] وأَن تَكونَ بِالعَرَبيَّةِ.

[٩] وأَن يُسمِعَها أَربَعينَ.

[١٠] وأَن تَكونَ كُلُّها في وَقتِ الظُهرِ.

The prerequisites for the two sermons are ten:
1. being pure from minor and major ritual impurification;
2. being pure from filth on one's clothes, body, and place;
3. covering one's nakedness;
4. standing – for someone who is able to do so;

5. sitting between the two sermons longer than one reposes during prayer;
6–7. consecutiveness between the two sermons and the prayer;
8. the sermon being in Arabic;
9. the forty hear it; and
10. it is performed in its entirety during the time of Noon Prayer.

Funerals

Obligations Toward The Deceased

(فَصلٌ) الذي يَلزَمُ لِلمَيِّتِ أَربَعُ خِصالٍ:
[١] غُسلُهُ.
[٢] وتَكفينُهُ.
[٣] والصَّلاةُ عَلَيهِ.
[٤] ودَفنُهُ.

The things required for the deceased are four types:
1. washing him,
2. shrouding him,
3. praying over him, and
4. burying him.

Washing

(فَصلٌ) أَقَلُّ الغُسلِ: تَعميمُ بَدَنِهِ بِالماءِ. وَأَكمَلُهُ: أَن يَغسِلَ سَوأَتَيهِ، وأَن يُزيلَ القَذَرَ مِن أَنفِهِ، وأَن يُوَضِّئَهُ، وأَن يُدَلِّكَ بَدَنَهُ بِالسِّدرِ، وأَن يَصُبَّ الماءَ عَلَيهِ ثَلاثًا.

The minimal washing is water covering his entire body.

The complete washing is:
- washing his buttocks,
- removing filth from his nose,
- performing ablution for him,
- rubbing his body with lote tree, and
- pouring water over him three times.

Shrouding

(فَصلٌ) أَقَلُّ الكَفَنِ ثَوبٌ يَعُمُّهُ.

وَأَكمَلُهُ لِلرِجُلِ ثَلاثُ لَفائِفَ.

وَلِلمَرأَةِ قَمِيصٌ وخِمارٌ وإزارٌ ولِفافَتانِ.

The minimal shroud is a [single] garment covering his entire body.

The complete shroud for a man is three sheets.

For a woman, it is:
- a long shirt [*qamīṣ*],
- a long head covering [*khimār*],
- a long waist covering [*izār*], and
- two sheets.

The Prayer

(فَصلٌ) أَركانُ صَلاةِ الجَنازَةِ سَبعَةٌ:

الأَوَّلُ: النِّيَّةُ.

الثَّاني: أَربَعُ تَكبِيراتٍ.

Funerals

الثَّالِثُ: القِيامُ عَلىٰ القَادِرِ.

الرَّابِعُ: قِراءَةُ الفاتِحَةِ.

الخامِسُ: الصَّلاةُ علىٰ النَّبِيِّ ﷺ بَعدَ الثَّانِيَةِ.

السَّادِسُ: الدُّعاءُ لِلمَيِّتِ بَعدَ الثَّالِثَةِ.

السَّابِعُ: السَّلامُ.

The essential elements of the Funeral Prayer are seven.

The first is the intention.

The second is four sayings of "*Allāhu akbar*."

The third is standing for those able to do so.

The fourth is reciting Al-Fātiḥah.

The fifth is supplicating upon the Prophet (may Allah bless him and give him peace) after the second ["*Allāhu akbar*"].

The sixth is supplicating for the deceased after the third ["*Allāhu akbar*"].

The seventh is saying, "*As-salāmu ʿalaykum*."

Burial

(فَصلٌ) أَقَلُّ الدَّفنِ: حُفرَةٌ تَكتُمُ رائِحَتَه وتَحرُسُهُ مِنَ السِّباعِ. وَأَكمَلُهُ: قامَةٌ وبَسطَةٌ، ويُوضَعُ خَدُّهُ علىٰ التُّرابِ، ويَجِبُ تَوجِيهُهُ إلىٰ القِبلَةِ.

The minimal burial is digging enough to conceal his odor and protect him from predators.

The complete burial is it being deep enough to stand inside with one's arms raised above.

His cheek is placed on the soil.

It is obligatory to face him towards the direction of prayer.

Exhumation

(فَصْلٌ) يُنبَشُ المَيِّتُ لأَربَعِ خِصالٍ:

[١] لِلغُسلِ إذا لَم يَتَغَيَّر.

[٢] لِتَوجيهِهِ إلىٰ القِبلَةِ.

[٣] لِلمالِ إذا دُفِنَ مَعَهُ.

[٤] لِلمَرأةِ إذا دُفِنَ جَنينُها مَعَها وأمكَنَت حَياتُهُ.

There are four reasons to exhume the deceased:
1. to wash [him] while he has not changed,
2. to face him towards the direction of prayer,
3. [to retrieve] money that was buried with him, and
4. a pregnant woman while it is possible that her fetus is alive.

Assistance

(فَصْلٌ) الاستِعاناتُ أربَعُ خِصالٍ:

[١] مُباحَةٌ.

[٢] وخِلافُ الأَولىٰ.

[٣] ومَكروهَةٌ.

[٤] وواجِبَةٌ.

Funerals

فالمُباحَةُ: هِيَ تَقريبُ الماءِ.
وَخِلافُ الأَولىٰ: هِيَ صَبُّ الماءِ علىٰ نَحوِ المُتَوَضِّئِ.
والمَكروهَةُ: هِيَ لِمَن يَغسِلُ أعضاءَهُ.
والواجِبَةُ: هِيَ لِلمَريضِ عِندَ العَجزِ.

The reasons for offering assistance [with water for purification] are four:
1. permissible,
2. best avoided,
3. offensive, and
4. obligatory.

The permissible is moving water closer.

The best avoided is pouring water for the likes of making ablution.

The offensive is helping someone perform ablution over their limbs.

The obligatory is helping a sick person [do the same] when they are not able.

Zakat

(فَصلٌ) الأموالُ التي تَلزَمُ فيها الزَّكاةُ سِتَّةُ أنواعٍ:

[١] النَّعَمُ.

[٢] والنَّقدانِ.

[٣] والمُعَشَّراتُ.

[٤] وأموالُ التِّجارَةِ؛ واجِبُها: رُبُعُ عُشرِ قِيمَةِ عُروضِ التِّجارَةِ.

[٥] والرِّكازُ.

[٦] والمَعدِنُ.

The categories of wealth from which zakat is obligatory are six:
1. livestock,
2. gold and silver coins,
3. "tenths" [i.e., raisins, dried dates, and grains],
4. trade-related wealth (its obligation is one-quarter of a tenth [2.5%] of the value of trade goods), and
5. buried treasure, and
6. ore.

Fasting

How It Becomes Obligatory

(فَصلٌ) يَجِبُ صَومُ رَمَضانَ بِأَحَدِ أُمورٍ خَمسَةٍ:

أَحَدُها: بِكَمالِ شَعبانَ ثَلاثينَ يَومًا.

وثانيها: بِرُؤيَةِ الهِلالِ في حَقِّ مَن رَآهُ، وإن كانَ فاسِقًا.

وثالِثُها: بِثُبوتِهِ في حَقِّ مَن لَم يَرَهُ بِعَدلِ شَهادَةٍ.

ورابِعُها: بِإخبارِ عَدلٍ رِوايَةً مَوثوقٍ بِهِ؛ سَواءٌ وَقَعَ في القَلبِ صِدقُهُ أَم لا، أو غَيرِ مَوثوقٍ بِهِ إن وَقَعَ في القَلبِ صِدقُهُ.

وخامِسُها: بِظَنِّ دُخولِ رَمَضانَ بِالاجتِهادِ فيمَن اشتَبَهَ عَلَيهِ ذَلِكَ.

Fasting Ramadan becomes obligatory via one of five matters.

The first is by completing thirty days of Shaʿbān.

The second is by sighting the new moon – for the person who saw it, even if they are morally corrupt.

The third is by it being established by an upright witness – for someone who did not see it

The fourth is by being informed by an individual who is trusted to transmit information and entrusted to do so – whether or not one believes it to be true. Or by being involved by an individual who is trusted – provided that one considers it to be true.

The fifth is by estimating that Ramadan has entered through personal reasoning – for someone to whom Ramadan's entry is unclear [such as one held in confinement].

Prerequisites for Its Soundness

(فَصلٌ) شُروطُ صِحَّتِهِ أَربَعَةُ أَشياءَ:

[١] إِسلامٌ.

[٢] وعَقلٌ.

[٣] ونَقاءٌ عَن نَحوِ حَيضٍ.

[٤] وعِلمٌ بِكَونِ الوَقتِ قابِلًا لِلصَّومِ.

The prerequisites for its soundness are four things:
1. being a Muslim;
2. of sound mind;
3. free of menstruation and its likes; and
4. knowing that the time is open for fasting.

Prerequisites for Its Obligation

(فَصلٌ) شُروطُ وُجوبِهِ خَمسَةُ أَشياءَ:

[١] إِسلامٌ.

[٢] وتَكليفٌ.

Fasting

[٣] وإِطاقَةٌ.

[٤] وصِحَّةٌ.

[٥] وإِقامَةٌ.

The preconditions for it being obligatory are five things:
1. being a Muslim,
2. legally responsible,
3. capable,
4. healthy, and
5. a resident [i.e., not traveling].

Essential Elements

(فَصلٌ) أركانُهُ ثَلاثَةُ أَشياءَ:

[١] نِيَّةٌ لَيلًا لِكُلِّ يَومٍ في الفَرْضِ.

[٢] وتَركُ مُفَطِّرٍ ذاكِرًا مُختارًا غَيرَ جاهِلٍ مَعذورٍ.

[٣] وصائِمٌ.

Its essential elements are three things:
1. an intention during the night for each obligatory day [of fasting];
2. omitting anything that breaks the fast out of remembrance and choice, without being ignorant or excused; and
3. the individual who fasts.

Missed Fasts

(فَصْلٌ) ويَجِبُ مع القَضاءِ لِلصّومِ الكَفَّارَةُ العُظْمَىٰ، والتَّعْزيرُ علىٰ مَن أفْسَدَ صَوْمَهُ في رَمَضانَ يَوْمًا كامِلًا بِجِماعٍ تامٍّ آثِمٍ بِهِ لِلصَّومِ.

وَيَجِبُ مع القَضاءِ الإمْساكُ لِلصّومِ في سِتَّةِ مَواضِعَ:

الأَوَّلُ: في رَمَضانَ – لا في غَيرِهِ – علىٰ مُتَعَدٍّ بِفِطْرِهِ.

والثَّاني: علىٰ تارِكِ النِّيَّةِ لَيْلًا في الفَرْضِ.

والثَّالِثُ: علىٰ مَن تَسَحَّرَ ظانًّا بَقاءَ اللَّيلِ فَبَانَ خِلافُهُ.

والرَّابِعُ: علىٰ مَن أفطَرَ ظانًّا الغُروبَ فَبانَ خِلافُهُ أيضًا.

والخامِسُ: علىٰ مَن بَانَ لَهُ يَومُ ثَلاثينَ شَعبانَ أنَّهُ مِن رَمَضانَ.

والسَّادِسُ: علىٰ مَن سَبَقَهُ ماءُ المُبالَغَةِ مِن مَضْمَضَةٍ واستِنشاقٍ.

In addition to making up the fast, performing a major expiation and discretionary discipline are obligatory for someone who spoiled a complete day of fasting during Ramadan provided intercourse is unlawful due to fasting itself.

Abstaining [from fast-breakers] is obligatory – in addition to making up the fast – in six contexts.

The first is during Ramadan (but not elsewhere) for someone whose breaks it is a transgression.

Fasting

The second is someone who omitted the intention during the night for an obligatory fast.

The third is someone who ate while thinking the night remains, but it turns out to be the opposite.

The fourth is someone who broke his fast while thinking that sunset had occurred, but it turns out to be the opposite.

The fifth is someone who, on [what he thinks is] the thirtieth day of Shaʿbān, finds out it is [the first of] Ramadan.

The sixth is someone who ingests water as a consequence of inhaling or sniffing excessively [during purification].

Invalidators

(فَصلٌ) يَبطُلُ الصَّومُ:
- بِرِدَّةٍ.
- وحَيضٍ ونِفاسٍ أو وِلادَةٍ.
- وجُنونٍ ولَو لَحظَةً.
- وبِإغماءٍ وسُكرٍ تَعَدَّى بِهِما إن عَمَّا جَميعَ النَّهارِ.

Fasting is invalidated by:
- apostasy;
- menstruation, postnatal bleeding or birth;
- insanity (even for an instant);
- losing consciousness and intoxication when they are themselves transgressions – provided they cover the entire daytime.

Breaking The Fast during Ramadan

(فَصلٌ) الإفطارُ في رَمَضانَ أَربَعَةُ أنواعٍ:

[١] واجِبٌ: كَما في الحائِضِ والنُّفَساءِ.

[٢] وجائِزٌ: كَما في المُسافِرِ والمَريضِ.

[٣] ولا ولا: كَما في المَجنونِ.

[٤] ومُحَرَّمٌ: كَمَن أَخَّرَ قَضاءَ رَمَضانَ مع تَمَكُّنِهِ حتَّى ضاقَ الوَقتُ عَنهُ.

The categories of breaking the fast during Ramadan are four.

Obligatory, like for a woman who is menstruating or has postnatal bleeding.

Permissible, like for someone who is traveling or sick.

Neither of the two, like someone who is insane.

Unlawful, like someone who delayed making up Ramadan – despite being able to do so – until the time becomes too short for it [i.e., the makeup].

Categories of Broken Fasts

وَأَقسامُ الإفطارِ أَربَعَةٌ أَيضًا:

أَوَّلُها: ما يَلزَمُ فيهِ القَضاءُ والفِديَةُ، وهوَ اثنانِ:

الأَوَّلُ: الإفطارُ لِخَوفٍ علىٰ غَيرِهِ.

والثَّاني: الإفطارُ مع تَأخيرِ قَضاءٍ مع إمكانِهِ حتَّى يَأتيَ رَمَضانٌ آخَرُ.

وَثانِيَها: ما يَلزَمُ فيهِ القَضاءُ دونَ الفِديَةِ، وهوَ يَكثُرُ؛ كَمُغمًى عَلَيهِ.

وَثالِثُها: ما يَلزَمُ فيهِ الفِديَةُ دونَ القَضاءِ، وهوَ: شَيخٌ كَبيرٌ.

ورابِعُها: لا ولا، وهوَ: المَجنونُ الذي لَم يَتَعَدَّ بِجُنونِهِ.

The divisions of breaking the fast are also four.

[The first] requires a make-up and an expiation. They are two [sub-divisions].

[The first sub-division is] breaking the fast out of fear for someone else.

The second [sub-division] is breaking the fast combined with delaying its make-up even though one was able to do so before the next Ramadan came.

The second [division] requires a make-up without a *fidyah*, and they are numerous – for example, someone who lost consciousness.

The third is requires a *fidyah* without a make-up. It is an elderly individual [who cannot fast].

The fourth requires neither. It is someone who is insane and whose insanity that does not result from a transgression.

What Does Not Break The Fast

(فَصلٌ) الذي لا يُفَطِّرُ مِمَّا يَصِلُ إلىٰ الجَوفِ سَبعَةُ أفرادٍ:

[١] ما يَصِلُ إلىٰ الجَوفِ بِنِسيانٍ.

[٢] أو جَهلٍ.

[٣] أو إكراهٍ.

[٤] وبِجَرَيانِ رِيقٍ بِما بَينَ أَسنانِهِ وقَد عَجَزَ عَن مَجِّهِ لِعُذرِهِ.

[٥] وما وَصَلَ إلىٰ الجَوفِ وكانَ غُبارَ طَريقٍ.

[٦] وما وَصَلَ إليهِ وكانَ غَربَلَةَ دَقيقٍ.

[٧] أو ذُبابًا طائِرًا أو نَحوَهُ.

The things that do not invalidate the fast even though they reach internal cavities are seven:

1–3. what reaches the abdomen out of forgetfulness, ignorance, or compulsion;
4. saliva passing over something stuck between his teeth that he is not able to spit out;
5. dirt in the path that reaches the abdomen;
6–7. particles of wheat being sifted, a flying fly, or the like reaching the abdomen.

واللَّهُ أَعلَمُ بِالصَّوابِ.

And Allah knows best what is right.

Concluding Remarks

نَسْأَلُ اللَّهَ الكَريمَ بِجاهِ نَبِيِّهِ الوَسيمَ أَن يُخرِجَني مِنَ الدُّنيا مُسلِمًا، وَوَالِدَيَّ وَأَحِبّائي، وَمَن إِلَيَّ انتَمَى، وأَن يَغفِرَ لي ولَهُم مُقحَماتٍ ولَمَمًا.

وصلَّى اللَّهُ عَلىٰ سيِّدِنا مُحَمَّدِ بنِ عَبدِ اللَّهِ بنِ عَبدِ المُطَّلِبِ بنِ هاشِمٍ بنِ عَبدِ مَنافٍ؛ رَسولِ اللَّهِ إلىٰ كافَّةِ الخَلقِ، رَسولِ المَلاحِمِ، حَبيبِ اللَّهِ، الفاتِحِ الخاتِمِ، وآلِهِ وصَحبِهِ أجمَعينَ. والحَمدُ لِلَّهِ رَبِّ العالَمينَ.

We beseech Allah the Generous, through the prestige of His graceful Prophet, to remove me from this world as a believer, and [to do likewise with] my parents, loved ones, and whoever is affiliated with me. And [we beseech Him] that He forgive me and them [for our] major and minor sins.

May the prayers of Allah be upon our master Muḥammad bin ʿAbd Allāh bin ʿAbd al-Muṭṭalib bin Hāshim bin ʿAbd Manāfin, the Messenger of Allah to the entirety of creation, the Messenger of engagements, the beloved to Allah who is the beginning and ending, and upon his folk and companions altogether. And praise is for Allah Lord of the worlds.

Detailed Table of Contents

PREFACE VIII

AUTHOR'S INTRODUCTION 1

BELIEFS 3
  The Pillars of Islam 3
  The Meaning of "There Is No Deity Other Than Allah" 4

PURIFICATION 5
  Physical Maturity 5
  Cleaning with Dry Objects 5
  Obligatory Actions of Ablution 6
  The Intention 7
  Large And Small Volumes of Water 8
  The Purification Bath 8
    Occasions That Require It 8
    Obligatory Actions of The Purificatory Bath 9
  Ablution 9
    Prerequisites for Ablution 9
    Invalidators of Ablution 11
  Things Unlawful Due to Impurification 12
    Due to Invalidated Ablution 12
    Due to Sexual Impurification 12
    Due to Menstruation 13
  Dry Ablution 14
    Causes 14

Detailed Table of Contents

    Conditions   15
    Obligatory Actions   16
    Invalidators   17
  Filth   17
    What Can Be Purified   17
    Categories   18
    How to Clean   18
  Menstruation   19

PRAYER   21
  Excuses   21
  Prerequisites   21
    Causes of Ritual Impurification   22
    Categories of Nakedness   23
  Performance   24
    Essential Elements   24
    Intention   25
    The Prerequisites for The Inaugural "Allāhu Akbar"   26
    Preconditions for Al-Fātiḥah   28
    Al-Fātiḥah's Doubled Letters   29
    Raising The Hands   31
    The Preconditions for Prostrating   31
    Limbs of Prostration   32
    Supplicating upon The Prophet ﷺ; Doubled Letters   34
    Minimum "As-Salāmu 'Alaykum"   35
    Prayer Times   35
    Times When It Is Unlawful To Pray   37
    Pauses for Silence   38
    Elements Requiring Reposing   38
    Causes of The Prostration of Forgetfulness   39
    The Greater Recommended Acts   40
    Prayer Invalidators   41
  Congregational Prayer   42

Ark of Salvation

    Conditions for Leading 42
    Conditions for Following 43
    Forms of Leading And Following 44
  Shortening And Joining Prayers 45
    The Conditions for Preemptive Joining 45
    The Conditions for Delayed Joining 46
    The Conditions for Shortening 46
  Friday Prayer 47
    Conditions for The Friday Prayer 47
    Essential Elements of The Sermons 48
    Prerequisites for The Sermons 49

FUNERALS 51
  Obligations Toward The Deceased 51
  Washing 51
  Shrouding 52
  The Prayer 52
  Burial 53
  Exhumation 54
  Assistance 54

ZAKAT 56

FASTING 57
  How It Becomes Obligatory 57
  Prerequisites for Its Soundness 58
  Prerequisites for Its Obligation 58
  Its Essential Elements 59
  Missed Fasts 60
  Invalidators 61
  Breaking The Fast During Ramadan 62
  Categories of Broken Fasts 62
  What Does Not Break The Fast 63

CONCLUDING REMARKS 65

Also from Islamosaic
Connecting to the Quran
Etiquette with the Quran
Infamies of the Soul
Hadith Nomenclature Primers
Hanbali Acts of Worship
Ibn Juzay's Sufic Exegesis
Refutation of Those Who Do Not Follow the Four Schools
Sharḥ Al-Waraqāt
Shaykh al-Sulamī's Waṣiyyah
Supplement for the Seeker of Certitude
The Accessible Conspectus
The Encompassing Epistle
The Evident Memorandum
The Ultimate Conspectus

www.islamosaic.com

This page left blank

www.ingramcontent.com/pod-product-compliance
Lightning Source LLC
Chambersburg PA
CBHW030159100526
44592CB00009B/355